MILAGRO

MILAGRO

Penelope Alegria

Haymarket Books
Chicago, Illinois

Published in 2020 by
Haymarket Books
P.O. Box 180165
Chicago, IL 60618
773-583-7884
www.haymarketbooks.org
info@haymarketbooks.org

ISBN: 978-1-64259-522-2

Distributed to the trade in the US through Consortium Book Sales and Distribution (www.cbsd.com) and internationally through Ingram Publisher Services International (www.ingramcontent.com).

This book was published with the generous support of Lannan Foundation and Wallace Action Fund.

Special discounts are available for bulk purchases by organizations and institutions. Please call 773-583-7884 or email info@haymarketbooks.org for more information.

Cover artwork by Joseph Lee. Joseph Lee is a self-taught artist who studies faces and the emotions that inhabit them. Lee focuses on the parallel between external reality and internal process by manipulating everyday faces and objects through segmented brush strokes, color choice, and volume, converging them into a complete and balanced whole. He is currently based in Los Angeles.

Cover design by Rachel Cohen.

Printed in the United States.

Library of Congress Cataloging-in-Publication data is available.

10 9 8 7 6 5 4 3 2 1

Contents

Self-Portrait as the Miracle My Parents Peg Me For

Milagro isn't just my middle name.
Milagro is a cavern echo
of my mom's womb,

empty even after a decade or so
of Lima's obstetrics
and Cook County Hospital.

For twelve years,
my dad hugged my mom after post-ops
and held her hand under fluorescent lights.

Twelve years of waiting rooms
would make a pincushion
out of any other woman,

but in every injection: hope;
in every surgery: faith;
in every stomach scar: a strong hand's resolve.

God knows the head nod of my mom's *padre nuestro,*
the crease of my dad's shut eyes
under the Ashland cathedral's stained Jesus glass.

Milagro
is the Spanish prayers
finally breaking through the clouds.

Milagro
is the epilogue
of my mom's nightly terror,

of her old fear
that her bloodline was dripping dry
like a leaky faucet.

8   My middle name is a birthmark,
some splotched skin my parents thumb
for record of God's will.

To see my parents' plane ticket to O'Hare,
the one-way they took in search of
hope and doctors and firstborns,

just grab my birth certificate.
To behold a debt that can never
be repaid, just say my full legal name.

Milagro is a three-syllable summary
of eternal expectation, an immortal tick
that bugs me to take the trash out,

to finish my science packet,
to wipe the tears after my friends fight,
but it's not overwhelming. I grew up sacred;

I was born with a halo.
We're all a miracle at some point,
and don't I know it.

La guitarra llora When My Parents Meet

Y al ver que inútilmente te envío mis palabras
llorando mi guitarra se deja oír su voz.

The day his brown eyes meet her brown eyes,
the guitar hustler sings an off-key song of poverty
as passengers swing on and off el micro,
the small green busses of Lima.
His jutting head stock sways with the melody,
serenading eyes that have learned to take no notice.

His brown eyes have learned to take no notice
as vendors shoulder their way through the jungle of limbs,
shouting, *tamarindo-chicha-choclo,*
competing with him for spare change.
The arms, legs, and heads crammed in el micro
sway as the small green bus swerves around missing manhole covers:
the putrid mist from open sewer lids wrinkles noses.

Amid the overcrowding, the hustlers, the vendors
her brown eyes have learned to take no notice,
so, on the way home from the hospital where she is a secretary,
when the sweet garbage stench washes in and
mixes with the body odor of the guitar hustler
shoving a jingling cup into her chest,
she looks over his black hair as the city lights blur past.

Her forehead glistens with humidity; droplets roll down her spine.
Her hair frizzes like blonde cotton candy.
Compressed in the aisle,
her sweaty knuckles brace her to the back of a seat,
and as the guitar hustler moves on, her stare slips,
and her brown eyes meet his brown eyes.

He's seen her get on. He's been waiting to say something,
thinking of the right words as he sings along.

10   She's the only blonde in a sea of brown,
      and in the jumble of legs and sweaty heads and jutting elbows,
      his brown eyes meet her brown eyes.
      She responds by pushing her way through the people
      to exit el micro,
      but there's something about her worth following.
      He shoulders past the tamarindo vendor,
      catches up to her on the street,
      grasps for her fingertips, and their eyes meet.

      The kiosk sells single cigarettes, and she doesn't even smoke,
      but there's something about him worth smoking for.

      She coughs, *cough-coughs.*
      Her brown eyes meet his brown eyes, and the
      question marks exhaled from her lungs
      hanging in the air between them
      become ellipses,
      which he flirts with:

      Cansado de llamarte, con mi alma destrozada
      comprendo que no vienes porque no quiere Dios,
      y al ver que inútilmente te envío mis palabras
      llorando mi guitarra se deja oír su voz…

Una canción del querer y no tener

for Sarah Montez

"¿Qué te importa que te ame si tú no me quieres ya?
El amor que ya ha pasado no se debe recordar.
Si las cosas que uno quiere se pudieran alcanzar,
tú me quisieras lo mismo que veinte años atrás."
—"Veinte años" por Bebo y Cigala

El mundo se pasa mitad del tiempo
construyendo muros,
y la otra mitad
tratando de tumbarlos.

Las estrellas esta noche
se organizan en figuras sin patrón,
como las de esa noche
como que no quieren formar tu cara
para no imaginarla.

Pero yo te imagino
caminando por una pista como esta
de cemento roto y trapos descosidos.

Aquí, la gente tira ropa vieja en la vereda
como si no supieran lo que es ser desnudo
y dejar el alma a los pies del mundo.

Yo te imagino
cuando camino por pistas como estas,
cuando veo polos rotos y pantalones desteñidos,
y si yo quisiera,
los amarraria con nudos de pescador
hasta que lleguen a tus veredas.

Tras las montañas y
el oceano pacifico,

12   bajo la luna gitana
construiria una cuerda de ropa vieja
para traerte a mi lado.

Las estrellas esta noche
se organizan en figuras sin patrón,
como las de esa noche
como que no quieren formar tu cara
para no imaginarla.

El mundo se pasa mitad del tiempo
construyendo muros,
y yo paso mi mitad
tratando de tumbarlos.

El barrio, or My Dad's Backbone

My dad is from
the specks of dirt in his beer,
born from the swaying hips of a Peruvian barrio
and its fog of heat by the stars that could fix
everything underneath. He says
el barrio had a constellation that he hasn't seen in twenty years,

a series of stars he hasn't seen since he moved out, back in his early years.
My dad is from
a house with a tin rooftop, says
back in his day, there was nothing the stars and a beer
couldn't fix
except for the neighbors, kissing the holy cross before housebreaking, in
          his barrio.

El barrio,
he says, has loosened road dust that crusts under fingernails for years,
dirt he couldn't scrape even when he left the block he couldn't fix.
My dad is from
old stories *wish-washing* at the bottom of his beer
and the salsa songs he can't sing, says

there's something about where he's from, says
"el barrio
has a filth that forever clouds your beer,
the kind that soils stories for the rest of your years.
I'm from
a crater of a city my favorite constellation couldn't fix.

I'm from a crater of a house whose roof I couldn't fix."
My dad remembers when he drinks, and that's all he says.
Four blocks worth of Jesus on chains and burglar friends is where he's
          from.
El barrio
is his fingernails' dirt, packed in even after all these years,
is the unleaving grime on the glass bottle of his beer.

14   I only know el barrio through what he tells me when he tips back his beer.
When he was young, my dad expected the stars to fix
all his years.
He looked up and waited and nothing ever changed, he says.
The roof was still tin, the road was still unpacked dust in his barrio.
What could he do but move out and shower away where he was from?

My dad is from the specks of dirt still whirling in his beer,
born from the swaying hips of el barrio, raised under a fog of heat by the
        stars that could fix
everything underneath. Says, he'd been wishing to live under a different
        sky for many, many years.

Amor de lejos amor de pendejos

Before my mother's wedding starts,
she's on the cathedral steps,
cigarette between her teeth as guests arrive,
smiling and nodding as she holds the door open.

Her mother is frantic hands,
reaching under handshakes and hello-kisses to
smooth dress wrinkles because white
doesn't give you anything to hide behind.
All hot breath as she *hmphs:*

don't let him out of your sight;
even a good man fucks
when you're not looking.

And in my mother's eyes:
a woman
who never learned to hug
without checking over the shoulder.

And in her mother's eyes:
a futuro already pisado,
a prophecy of her daughter, too
washing collars with red lipstick residue:
an obligation she'll inherit like a house chore.

There's no response.
Only a cigarette drag
as my mother leans
against the cathedral wall.

My Mom's Hands Come to Chicago, Winter of '99

I.

Her last day in Lima is a goodbye party. Aunts, uncles, cousins, and teenagers from el barrio sit encircled in white plastic chairs. On the patio, the bottle glows yellow under the streetlight's circle as they pass a Dixie cup of beer between dirty fingernails. Inside the house, her hands sort through her suitcase for the eighth time, checking for American dollars, shampoo, chocolate: the scales of her palms weigh the need of ponchos knitted by tia versus cloth dolls from her childhood. She takes her framed college diploma out of her suitcase to make more room; it won't translate in America. When mama calls her from the kitchen, she walks into papa's arms; his beer breath meets her with *mi hijita, mi hijita, mi hijita.* Everyone on the patio watches them: the beer stops passing. She curls her fingers into his hair knowing this won't travel through the telephone. She wishes she could wrap mama's smile and papa's hands in aluminum foil, tuck them under the cloth dolls so security won't catch them in the scanner.

Mama swats a greasy rag at them; she needs help serving the ceviche.

II.

In December Chicago, she's on Olga's doorstep.

She thumbs the small black plaque reading *Aguilar,*
knuckles white as her breath.

Her teeth chatter in a poncho and sandals: toes numb from snow.

The floor creaks as she sets down her suitcase,
arms goosebumped in Spanish wrap around her cousin.

Olga says she can sleep on the air mattress on the kitchen floor.

Trading the comfort of Lima
for unknown Chicago seems a mistake now.

How many days will this kitchen be her bedroom?

Olga tells her not to mind the drip of the soggy ceiling,
or the dirge of winter whistling through the window,

but she needs to find a warmth like Lima's.

No cloth doll from tia will take away her hunger and doubt,
but she can feed one to take care of the other.

100 papas rellenas should sell for $300.

She soaks the potatoes first, peeling and mashing them.

She flattens potato dough into a disk and into each scoops
three tablespoons of ground beef, two olives, half a hard-boiled egg;

drops them into the frier.

She walks between cars stopped on North Broadway and Wilson,
and the tray of papas rellenas sells out in two hours.

Make. Sell. Repeat. Make. Sell. Repeat. Make. Sell. Repeat.
North Broadway and Wilson becomes a thousand dollars a week, and

the dirge of winter crossfades into a psalm of spring as Chicago begins to
         take root.

When I Visit Peru for the First Time, My Dad's Face is Everywhere

Long lost country that's not mine.
I cross the Equator into a city
blinking streaks of streetlight yellow
and puddles in holed cement
rippled by cousins I don't know,
little kids lapping to the dirty water's shore.

They laugh and I almost recognize them,
these cousins on sidewalk edges with fast words
hurdling over the jungle gym roof of their mouths.
I almost think them simple children
when they talk of girl wearing diamonds
and girls wearing diamonds in this city
of golden pavement.

I almost call these cousins mine. I almost reach for the phone
because the little boys have started whipping dripping mud
balls and my lips are wet from someone's under-the-bed
cerveza and you should see them because I know
these aren't my city's lights to be falling in love with.

I Eavesdrop on Family Gossip: It's Funny Until It's Not

The crack in my window
breaks the steady stream of night.
I trace the moonlight shards
on my navy blanket
to the metronome
of abuelita's consonants,
clicking after one another
like hurried high heels.

Cuando
Mari
played that
music,
Dios mio,
d'you see
Olga's
head shake?

The gossip pulses
through my room
like a two-step tango.

I squint at my window
hard enough to almost see
the cracks splintering outwards,
a rippling pond of glass.

Mama and Papa laugh
a belly-holding howl, loud
like a busy bar on Friday night.
I've heard that laugh before,
on our first Fourth of July
on the beach.

20 I remember watching people in the distance
    playing Frisbee in the moon's wavy reflection.
    After I came back to our spread blankets,
    crying because I couldn't bathe in the moon,
    my parents laughed like that too.
    I went home that night with a starry towel
    and no moon water.

    Abuelita munches on saltines
    for so long I almost fall asleep
    and miss her saying,
    "*Y esa niña?*
    Ya tienes que disciplinarla.
    Teach her how to boil water, y ya."

    I get so hot,
    I throw the blanket off.
    I frown at the beckoning window
    that won't stop splitting into spiderwebs,
    that crackles like a bonfire
    until I get sick of the noise
    and put my foot through it.

I Still Have a Sour Spot for Samantha

because she could play computer games all day
and she had a dog
we could walk around the block without a leash
and there was always soda in her fridge
so when she said *Santa isn't real*
I didn't stop coming to her house
even though her sister pulled my hair
and threw rice and blamed me
for breaking the good cups
because our moms had been pregnant together
because she had an upper lip scar and I wanted a cool mouth
because she was the only girl I knew who spoke Spanish
and had her own keys to the house
I didn't tell my parents
until five Christmases after
when I compared Mom's handwriting
to Santa's and it's not like I was
devastated or mad or traumatized
just sour like almost-ripe cherries
because Samantha told on me
called me *butterfingers* to her mom
when I didn't even break the good cups.

Her sister did.

If I Had Met My Childhood Hero

Girl on fire.
Daughter of coal.
Hunter of lamb and lover of stew.
You, Katniss Everdeen, were my fifth-grade obsession.

Katniss, why don't you come into my kitchen?
Clear the counter: we're making empanadas with my mom.

She'll teach you how to fold dough
while I season the chicken with rocoto peppers.
With Hector Lavoe shaking the tiles, we'll dance
until we run out of dough or oil or plates to pile empanadas on.

Once the house smells like garlic, I'll ask,
"How are the kids? Does Peeta still bake?
Could he beat my cooking if he tried?"
I know everything I need to know
about you and the revolution, Katniss.
Let's spread out blankets in my backyard.

I have to warn you: my mom will sometimes speak Spanish.
When she turns to pick lint off my leggings
and says, "te dije ayer que lavaras la ropa,"
don't be offended; she's not talking about you.
Instead, point out Sagittarius to us.
We don't know any constellations, but
we'll try to look for it after you leave.
We'll scan the sky and turn to each other and think of you.

You don't need to talk about your scars
or the herbal significance of your name
or how you chose between Gale and Peeta
even though the bread baker was a no-brainer.

My mom does want you to take these empanadas home, though.
Remember: the soft ones are for the kids.

Chui

I met you at Wisconsin Dells

waiting in line for the Hurricane water slide

Chewy like the granola bar I crunch for breakfast

you're my dad's oldest brother from Venezuela

your given name is Ricardo

but you chose this two note calling

these syllables my tongue stretches like pink bubblegum

Chui is what my dad yelled when your inflatable toppled in the pool

Chui is what I gasped when I pulled you up

and grazed your stub of a ring finger

sliced off before the first joint

ending awkwardly like a teenager ordering french fries

you sung me an explanation later

over a tuna sandwich on a plastic reclined chair

a ballad of looking for a half limb

in between couch legs in a furniture factory in Caracas

I rolled your scarred dome of skin between my fingers

until you napped to the roar of gushing water and running sandals

24

until you snored in the waterpark's sun

damning the saw for taking your finger

as you slept

The Night Before Moving
Out of Rogers Park

Mama's cooking banana empanadas in the kitchen
while Papa and I stuff my shorts into boxes
but I don't care about labeling cartons.
I'm waiting for the door to creak
and my uncle to walk through.

My uncle ate with us every morning,
crawled up from the basement
for Mama's breakfast omelette.
He'd pick off the mushrooms,
slide them onto my plastic plate:
here, they're slippery,

but the door doesn't creak
until four hours later.
My uncle slinks in,
side-stepping the boxes
to reach the oven's smell.

Papa swats a rag at his tardiness;
he was supposed to have helped,

but I run at him, a blur of ribboned sandals slapping tiles,
begging him to take me to the park one more time, *porfa please please.*
He says *yes, duh, little girls shouldn't be around so many boxes.*
He grabs some blackberries and I drag him to the swings.

The night's sour like tamarindo
as my uncle and I find our oak tree.
We lay in its cashew shadow,
looking at the half-moon, sucking on sour berries.
The sprouting weeds around our heads:
a constellation in the dark grass.

26   He sucks on a blackberry and burps.
I suck on a blackberry and cry
because I know this is a goodbye walk.
This is the last time I'll be at this park
with my uncle and his food.
When I move tomorrow, all I'll have
of his soft hands is this park memory
I'll remember in the mornings,
when I cut into Mama's breakfast omelette
because Papa likes his mushrooms,
he stabs each of them with a fork,
and if he eats his entire omelette,
who will give me mushrooms then?

For My Only Living Grandparent, Who I Only Remember Sometimes

I called abuelita this morning,
mostly because Papa told me to
and she'll be ninety-eight next month
and there's nothing to do on the highway without an AUX
and even old ladies know the emptiness of an answering machine.

She calls me Bubu
and remembers me at six,
slapping bandaids on my forehead
before walking to Dominick's.
And the 99 cent bagels
we'd eat? Breakfast, lunch, and dinner
on Saturdays? The store by the park
down the street. We made a day
out of that back-and-forth:
park, bagels, park, bagels.
You loved that aluminum slide,
always hot with summer sun.
And those cool swings.

I laugh and abuelita asks
why I don't call more often,
pearlita, amor de mi vida, mi razon de ser,
and I don't answer, just say,
abuelita mia,
until the highway ends and I hang up
before she can ask:

Why don't you love me?
Don't you know I'll be gone soon
and it'll be too late for phone calls?
Is that what you're waiting for?
The emptiness of an answering machine,
an absence that beeps with memory

28 *like suddenly craving bagels on Saturdays*
    after that damn Dominick's
    closed up shop and left?

I Spend an Entire Summer in my Lincolnwood Room

The sun from under my door
reflects a mirage off the hardwood.
My room could be on water
or in Paris, France. I wouldn't know.
I haven't poked my head out
since I moved to the suburbs
and realized I had nowhere to go
until school starts.

From my bed, I stare at the smokescreened sky
until I'm bored and trace the cracks in the plaster.
Here is the cement's cursive, the slitted river that peels
with my thumb. On my desk is my favorite smudge.
The wood's scars don't need ointment, just more
wet coffee mugs and empty water bottles
to crease the furniture.

This is the corner I dance in,
the only floorboard I don't shush at night,
the only piece of ground that won't gossip
about my big toes. What can I say? This flooring
taught me to be loud. This groaning cabinet
taught me to complain. At the end of the day,
I criss-cross at the edge of my bed and listen
to my room hum, the furnace's sigh,
the breath of this space whistling
me a goodnight lullaby.

Papa's Deli Order

When my social studies teacher spoke of DREAMERS and visas,
she said undocumented was a synonym for illegal.
My hand shot up to tell her she must be mistaken:
My parents were undocumented, and
my papa was no criminal.

On weekends, I help him with the deli order at Jewel.
I point out verses on the posters behind the counter:
> *Yo quiero cuarto de libra de Sarah Lee Honey Turkey.*
> *I want a quarter pound of Sarah Lee Honey Turkey.*
> *Yo quiero media libra de Queso Americano.*
> *I want a half pound of American cheese.*

I walk him through each word,
but he gets stuck on the *r*'s and the *s*'s—
he says he hears English like hissing radio static,
but I need him to walk up to the deli counter and order American cheese
because criminals don't eat American cheese.

When my father is pulled over on 69th street,
passengers huddle in the backseat of his Uber
as red stars, blue shirts, and badges
float in the grey sky outside.
Silhouetted against the city of big shoulders,
my father's big shoulders knot against their hissing English.

I miss nineteen of his calls
because I'm at school at debate practice.
After the March sun has set, I finally call back,
but I am too late.

The passengers have been Ubered by someone else.
He sits on the cold, concrete curb while
policemen hiss radio static, open compartments, turn over seat cushions,
and all my father hears is,

> *car,*
> *license.*

They say,

exit,

and he thinks the country,
he thinks expired visa,
he thinks goodbye hugs and tears at O'Hare
and returning to his mother's house in Peru,
to the yellow streetlights of the barrio he grew up in.

When I finally call back,
I want him to put the cops on the phone.
I want to tell them he only drives Uber on the weekends,
to tell them he's on his way to pick me up,
to tell them he can order a pound of American cheese for 1.99 at the deli
and that is important because criminals don't eat American cheese.

Instead, I tell my father,

Yo siempre estoy contigo.
Vamos a Panda Express cuando regreses a casa,
podemos conversar sobre pollo de naranja.
Let's go to Panda Express when you get home,
we can talk about it over orange chicken,
but when we go to the deli this weekend,
you have to order.
¿Como se dice? Dime.

He says,

I want a quarter pound, uh, Sarah Lee Honey Turkey.
The blue and white lights fade,
and he turns the key in the ignition.

I want de half pound of cheese American.
And under the yellow streetlights,
he starts home.

I Think I Left the Stove On

My palms are always clammy
as I slide my key into the lock,
as I turn it clockwise one click left
and the door creaks open to the kitchen
that has not yet burned down,
that doesn't have an ankle-deep pool of ashes
or thick smoke blackening the cabinets.

Instead, crusts of french toast are still on the cutting board;
oil from the morning's eggs dots the stovetop;
two knives and a spoon soak in a coffee mug's dirtied water.

I kiss the countertop when I come home
because the house smells like cinnamon
instead of something burning.
I lay lips on cream formica
because my kitchen and I are tight like that.
The house is quiet except for the furnace
and the cats on the Marshalls' calendar eyeballing me
like the spotlight of God does when nobody's home,
that circle of brightness that shines down
when it's quiet, and you feel somebody watching.

I run my pointer finger
across the stove's knobs to make sure it's off.
I shake the toaster plug to make sure it's not in the outlet.
The pressure cooker asks, *why don't you leave the stove on,
just to see what it does?*

To no one, do I admit my fear of fire.
To no one, do I ask,
is the house burning? as I pull out of the driveway.
I rationalize it on my way to school, like
*it's fine, it's fine, it's fine,
it's fine if the house burns down.*

Truth be told, a little big fire wouldn't hurt
anyone but my landlord.
A little smoke would only remind me
of how my mouth tastes like iron
when I'm scared, so, to no one
do I explain my fear of burning the house down,
though my kitchen and the calendar cats
know very well
how I feel.

A Scrapbook of My Favorite Moments

for S & F, my best friends

You burp out the window before you run a stop sign. / You read feminist theory at Mariano's and smear blue gelato on the cover. / You grab an extra glazed donut from your math class party just for me. / I take your neon EQUALITY crewneck from your locker because you gave me your combo. / I always have extra pairs of socks for when your feet get cold at my house. / You're the first warm day in March that suns the crown of my head. / You're the tupperware I keep your mother's biryani in. / You nap on my laminated periodic table sheet after failing another practice test. / You call shotgun wrong. You have to wait to see the car before you call it, you know. / For my birthday, you gift me Reese's and cucumber lotion. / You buy me iced coffee from Dunkin' when school has a late start. / You, snorting through yoga: the best cardio. / You say *pull up* during AP Lit discussions when you're losing the *Jane Eyre* sucks debate. Someday, someone will fist fight over literature, and what will I have to do then? / My love for you is the tree's uprooting of asphalt. / My love for you is the crumbled granola bits at the bottom of the bag. / When I want to share my epiphany, I FaceTime you until you wake up. / When I cry, you lay your cheek on my shoulder pillow and unthread the swarm of gargled sobs. / You're the only one I send videos of babies eating bananas. / You're the only one I love even when you forget to hold the door. / You're the only one I love even when you let a spider crawl in through the hole in my window. / You're the only one I love even when, after hearing me snore all night, you smack me awake with a pillow in the morning.

Aidan Doesn't Talk Politics on Vacation

Things were different for Aidan, so when Amnesty International explained their human rights work in Venezuela, he leaned in, whispered, *listen, I know this is important, but I don't want to talk about politics on vacation,* even though we were only in Brussels because we'd signed up to study world government, but things were different, so he couldn't tell how my skin grew too hot to hold, how I blamed the spicy mayo on Belgian fries and didn't reach for the Tabasco for five dinners straight, and because things were different, I didn't show him the boiling of my skin, I just bit my lip, unhinged my retainer and my second tongue and doused them in clorox, and because things were different, I didn't whisper back, I didn't tell him about my uncle wandering empty supermarket aisles in Caracas, and I didn't ask about Aidan's hungry relatives, I just picked on my callouses, and, as Amnesty International wrapped up their presentation, I left on the table a Granny Smith peel of me.

Open Letter to My Freshman Self

When a boy tells you he loves you for the first time
in a text message you read between biology and gym,
tell him mama made pan al horno for breakfast:
The goat cheese melted into the fresh-baked bread perfectly.

Because it is 8:53 AM on a Tuesday, and
it is too early in the day and too early in your life
to worry about three little words
when you have laps to run,
and that's dreadful enough without your tongue
tucked between your esophagus and your molars.

In study hall,
when he swears he'll give you Algebra homework,
when he talks of his father's medicine cabinet
and the time he tried to kill himself,
do not try to piece together his broken beer bottle ego.
You will slice your fingertips to ribbons,
and over years of washing dishes, the scars will rust.

When he is blowing smoke rings
in the back of his mother's grey Honda,
do not say I love you back.
Say, "I like tracing the Little Dipper in your palm."

When he calls you that night,
listen to him talk about mommy issues and alcohol,
how aliens put us on the planet, and we are their lab rats.
Interrupt him.
Tell him you love
beef pad thai and crab rangoon
and microwaved chicken ramen.

When he tells you he loves you in a text,
you know a morning "I love you" is different
from an afternoon one,

and an afternoon "I love you" is different from a hospital,
and you may be loud but there is no ambulance in your lungs—
that is not your job.
Do not sprinkle his sad stories on your toothpaste.
Do not make the mirror worry how to get love out of your molars.

So, when it is 8:53 AM on a Tuesday,
and he texts you he loves you for the first time,
tell him you're craving spaghetti and meatballs.
Tell him there's a southbound train to Kankakee this afternoon.
Tell him you are allergic to amoxicillin—
you get hives all over your belly.

Remember: he never asks
whether you are a cloud person or a star person.
He never asks what you order at Dunkin'.
He never asks if you'd rather
have fingers for toes or toes for fingers.
He only tells you what he wants.

Tell him about the apartment you want to own one day,
by the water so the beach will lull you to sleep.
You can smell fish and sand and sea.
Tell him your bedroom windows are painted *Starry Night*
and you wake up every morning with blue sun spilled over you.

You make coffee, take it on the beige suede couch,
and there's just no room for him on it.
You're busy waiting for Odysseus's ship to sail in
because he knows how to make pan al horno just right,
just like mama does.

You Will Not Work Like a Donkey: Portrait of My Mom's Worry

After Charles White's "Mother (Awaiting His Return)"

The slaughterhouse looms between
the sea and the sunrise, is there before
the day calls; when your *art* doesn't
pick up the phone bill; when you trot
toward the bus and grey cow intestines;
I know; your *art* doesn't need electricity
until after it's shut off, hears the hum
of heat when it's finally cold and the
factories are closed; your *art* forgets on
purpose; before I moved here, before
I met your dad, I used to live with the
animals; I fed the rooster and walked
the dog; I sat in a cart and made the
donkey pull; I left the slaughterhouse
because I hated killing animals, slitting
their throats and peeling their skin; I
know; everything is bright when you're
young and getting paid, but one of
these days, you'll be old and can't sleep
in; one of these days, there won't be
running water to wash off the dirt and
crusting blood under your fingernails.

I left the slaughterhouse, but one of
these days, you'll recognize its dawn
shadow; I know; when your *art* doesn't
cut it anymore, you'll know what it is
to clock in and step on a chicken head;
you'll know what it is to clock out and
know the mule
is next.

I Read an Interview with Tania, Speaking on Suegra Rosa on the Commute Home

The bodies of Salvadoran Òscar and his two-year-old daughter Angie were found on the Rio Grande's riverbank and recorded on camera. His wife, Tania, saw her family drown before returning to her mother-in-law's home.

Guiso. Guiso de carne y cebolla
was the last thing Rosa made
before knowing the river's hunger,
back when she could still talk,
trudge to the clothing factory.
La situación was never so bad
for that woman. Idle hands make
for the devil's playground and
an empty fridge. At least
we were working. Now,
my mother-in-law can't get off the sofa,
doesn't move anything except
her fingers to stroke
Angie's Disney Princess Blanket
like it's her hair.
Doesn't eat anything except
canchita, grinds her teeth on
hard corn like she hopes
it'll dislocate her jaw.
How do I feed a woman
who doesn't want her mouth?
She prays
to die and sinks
into Angie's sofa even after
I've seen death in the water,
watched mija y mi marido
get swallowed by the current.

40   Fourteen hours sowing belts
      didn't prick my hands helpless
      like the Big River did,
      flooding Oscar's mouth
      two strokes from the border.

      Rosa, give me back
      the graveyard shift. Won't you
      return being five cents short at the market.
      I want to be hungry again.
      I want an empty plate for dinner
      if there'll be four of us at the table.
      I know that's all you see:
      your son and nieta's blackened body
      splashed across every newsstand.
      I know you look at me
      and hear your warning:

      No te vayas.
      No te vayas.
      No te vayas.

No More Nuts Here

After Natalie Diaz's "No More Cake Here"

When ICE knocks the door down,
I panic, shriek, *let me*
get the cashews from the pantry
because I love cashews,
though Mom only eats almonds
and nuts give Dad gas.
I should've grabbed napkins,
but I thought the ICE carnival would supply.
I didn't cry about it
until I was in the back of ICE's red pickup,
squirming on prickling hay bales,
crammed between giant toddlers
and cholos with sweet taffy mouths.

ICE's deportation parade
trumpets out of the Chicago suburbs
and into Logan Square.
Onboard, there are bearded ladies
and three clowns crowding the passenger seat
and plastic pink dogs ballooning to the sky.
Loose hay needles pour out from the back
of ICE's red pickup as we prod through the city.
The toddlers fuss for food and grow twenty feet tall.
I'm bored, so I have Dad hum boleros.
I give Mom my cashews, but only five at a time.
That way, no one notices my Ziploc bag
forever bubbling more cashews,
and I'll have enough nuts to last me
until we reach desert or border officer
or whichever brands me brown first.

Uncle spots the giant toddlers
from his apartment and follows ICE's truck,
coos up at the balloon dogs like, cool clouds,

clasps his hands behind the
Eighth Wonder of the Modern World.
We draw quite a crowd.
Everyone swoons over our hayride and
abnormal babies until they get close
enough to smell the hay. Then, they yell, *oh,
so stinky!* and throw perfume bottles
and boo when we duck. Mom extends
five of her cashews anyways, as a thank you.
I slap her wrist and say, *no more nuts here.*
The toddlers and I pick at the hairy lady's
beard and flick her strands at the tourists.

ICE notices the carnival we've turned into
and tells the clowns in the passenger seat to shoot.
I force my cheek against the truck bed.
I force Dad to hum louder.
I force the cholos' sticky mouths to join
the choir without telling them the song.
Only happy *dun-dun-dun-dun* Saturday songs here.
Together, we sound like the little bells
and rollercoasters we're supposed to be.
The big little kids cry until they see
revolvers hanging from the driver's window.
This reminds us all of our cousins,
so for now, everyone is happy
to have a melody to strain.

ICE is hungry and makes everyone empty their pockets.
Pounds of pesos, receipts, gum, hair ties, lint,
and a sketch of La Virgen haloed by English prayer
fall. One officer tears my Social Security card
but not my magic bag of cashews, gracias a Dios.
After that, we wrap corn dogs of everything inutil and inedible,
whip cotton candy out of our pocket litter.
We look to the pink balloon clouds for redemption, stick each other with
        kisses
until a twenty-foot toddler sneezes away our family heirlooms.

We are half-a-quarter country from the Chihuahuan Desert
when Mom takes away my nuts de mierda.
She says I shouldn't hog the cashews, don't I see
all the kids here? She says this transcontinental truck
is shit, that deportation isn't a hayride and I've dreamed it all;
we were still home; ICE hadn't even come. The worst part is
that I'm a citizen. The worst part is that I dream of ICE raids
when I can't be raided. The worst part is that
I wake up every day under clean bedsheets. I think she's right,
but maybe the worst part is that I'm still waiting for the door
to be knocked down, the worst part is that
I can still taste the unbrushable cashew tang.

About the Author

Penelope Alegria is the 2019 Chicago Youth Poet Laureate and a three-time member of Young Chicago Authors' artistic apprenticeship, Louder Than a Bomb Squad. Her work has been featured or is forthcoming in *La Nueva Semana, El Beisman, Muse/A Journal, The Breakbeat Poets Vol. 4: LatiNEXT,* as well as BBC Radio 4 and WBEZ Radio Archives. She is a Brain Mill Press Editor's Pick, and was awarded the 2018 Literary Award by Julian Randall and both the 2019 and 2020 Poetry Award by the Niles West english department. She has performed spoken word at the Obama Foundation Summit, Pitchfork Music Festival, and other venues in the Chicagoland area. She will attend Harvard College in the fall of 2020.

Printed in the USA
CPSIA information can be obtained
at www.ICGtesting.com
JSHW012057140824
68134JS00035B/3491